the CRAZY world of SEX

Cartoons by
David Pye

≡EXLEY

"This yours?"

"STOP! STOP! One of my lenses is missing!"

"She asked me if I'd ever think of taking advantage of a woman who'd had too much to drink. I said 'No' ... I think she's gone home."

"See? I told you you could manage it without your medallions!"

'I bet Robert Redford never takes his pants off before his shirt ...'

"That's it then? Another cliff-hanger?"

"What's he like? Just like his car – noisy, overdecorated and very difficult to stop!"

"No the earth hasn't moved ... I've got cramp."

"No, I think I prefer the gorilla suit after all ..."

"Don't worry, looks don't mean much. And in your case nothing at all!"

"Don't sulk. You asked me what I wanted and I told you
– an egg, sunny side up."

"Sorry dear – did you say something? I must have dozed off …"

"O.K. I get it – sex is out. But can't we still be friends?"

"What do you mean 'My God, my husband'. I am your husband."

"An apple? You drag me all the way into this undergrowth for an apple?"

"No of course I don't mind sharing you with your teddy.
Goodness gracious me!"

"*There, I promise, Teddy won't see a thing!*"

"You're right. That is impossible. The book's upside down."

"Don't be alarmed officer, it's only my husband.
He likes to kerb crawl and offer me mint humbugs.
It's the only thing that can get him going these days."

"That looks like a hairpiece too!"

"For heaven's sake Trevor – I've still got my rucksack on!"

"I seem to remember you saying our foreplay was becoming rather predictable ... well ..."

"I should have warned you – Creme Caramel works like an aphrodisiac on Susan."

"Put this on, and a plastic bag over your head,
and I could just fancy you ..."

"Wow! You look exhausted. Have the kids been difficult?"

"But I don't want to sit in the back.
I want to stay here, with you!"

"*Excuse me my lord, but I think you're only supposed to kiss her ...*"

"Oi! Can't you read?"

"You a virgin yet?"

"Angela! Do you recall inviting the Polkinhams for
Trivial Pursuits this evening ...?"

"You used to moan about the lack of room. Now, when we can afford a big car, you want to go home!"

"Can I examine them more closely?"

"Yes, very nice but when I said why don't we dress up,
that's not quite what I meant."

"For goodness sake Doreen! Not now!"

"Do go on Mrs Spotwick – you were telling me your husband has no sense of time or place …

"My mother would absolutely kill me if she could see me now!"

"I know you haven't done anything, but if I bop you one <u>now</u>, you're not likely to, are you?"

"Hi! Remember last night and how you said my Porsche had
no bearing on our relationship?"

"No honestly ... You are the most beautiful girl in the world."

"When I say 'Penny for your thoughts' you could lie, instead of saying 'I wonder who won the football'!"

"I'm very worried about that boy ..."

"Why don't I turn the light out then you can stop holding your breath and let your tummy out?"

"Sorry darling, that's how it is with me – fake cannon, fake orgasm!"

"And all you want to do is _eat_ it? That's weird!"

"I've told you Wayne, either Teddy goes or I do!"

"My mother's told me about boys like you – but I never thought I'd find one!"

"*Relax mother – nobody's going to molest her – looking like that!*"

"And you can leave your pants on! It's going to take a lot more than a box of chocolates!"

"I'm going to sue them!"

"I don't know why you waste your money buying books like that when the real thing's so much funnier."

"Get in quickly, you clash horribly with the new quilt."

"To be honest, I'd rather you faked it instead of finishing your book half-way through!"

"O.K., I'm a bird, you're a bee. Where do we start?"

"*Well, go on, what about my knees?*"

"Forget Cinderella, I'm off to find the owner of this!"

"NO! NO! It's my heart – don't let them out!"

"Helping you on with your socks afterwards does rather take the edge off it!"

"'Course I know there's more to a relationship besides sex.
There's ...... er ...... and, er ......"

"What have I done to deserve this? Oh yes, I remember ..."

"Yes, you're right, foreplay is fun!"

"Aren't we supposed to scream and run away?"

"Nervous? Who's nervous?"

"What's a bit of a rash? – it's got a really sexy smell!"

"Oh all right ... but only during the breaks."

*"Don't get the idea I leap into <u>bed</u> with every man I meet ...
Heavens no – I'll <u>do</u> it anywhere!"*

"Same old story, I'm afraid. She said 'Penny for your thoughts',
I told her, she hit me and left."

"It says in my magazine that a lot of men
prefer a cigarette afterwards ..."

"*You can be honest with me – your heart's not really in this, is it?*"

"And don't pat me afterwards. It makes me feel married."

"That one doesn't count."

"Ingook, I love you ... er ... that is Ingook?"

"And in the very near future I see you needing dental treatment unless you take your hand off my knee ..."

"Isn't this fantastic? – Just you, me and the night!"

"*Just because you're good-looking with loads of money & a Porsche & fun to be with doesn't mean ... Oh, I don't know though!*"

"Well all right, but not here – nobody
can see us!"

"O.K. Casanova – I know you're in there."

"Just think! Now that my voice has broken, I'll be able to buy my own contraceptives!"

"Now I see it written down, I'm not so sure ..."

"You'll see – wait till it stops thrashing about – it's got at least eight legs!"

"Headache? What is 'headache'?"

"You mean that all these years you've just been <u>pretending</u>
to like my pre-lovemaking trombone solo?"

"But Daddy, we hadn't really started yet."

"I've just had a fantastic idea for your thesis! And, we could do all the experiments right here!"

"It's my turn Sarge – you haven't let me creep up and bang
on the roof all night!"

"Please excuse George. He gets these sudden urges!"

"Other women just get headaches ..."

"And no jiggling up and down – you'll wake them up."

"Hey girls! Look what I just invented – it'll drive the boys crazy!"

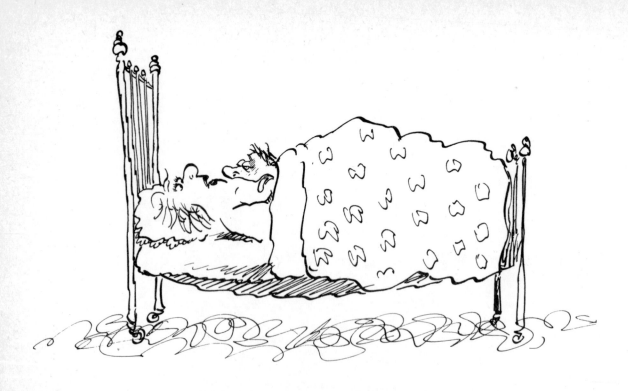

"Perhaps you'd like a bit of a rest."